# ANGER

Who gives a shite?

# DEREK O'NEILL

ORIGINAL WRITING

Editors: Nancy Moss
Front Cover Drawing: © 2012 by Diogenes Mezzadra

## Acknowledgment

*To all who read this book, I salute you for wanting to change the way you live for the better and for having the courage to be who you are as fully as possible.*

*To all who encourage me everyday to keep going and sharing their lives with me, family small and large. But most of all the little angel who came to teach me – Alexa, my granddaughter.*

# CONTENTS

*"Everybody hurts sometimes, and when we do it is nice to have Derek O'Neill around. His excellent little books on the things that get us, (fear, anger, depression, victimhood, mental blocks) allow us to find our way safely through our psychological minefields and arrive safely at the other side. Read them when you need them."*

- Paul Perry,
Author of the New York Times Bestseller
*Evidence of the Afterlife*

## Introduction

Everyone experiences anger. It's just a fact of life. People stand in our way or misunderstand us. Situations don't work out. Things seem unfair. Then we get angry. Instead of fighting the feeling and suppressing emotions, consider the value in just letting them fly. Maybe your anger needs to speak its mind.

We tend to fear our anger, as if it will hurt us to truly connect with it. There are times you just have to indulge and express anger. There's usually a good reason you feel it, and if you fight it, it will only grow and fester, hurting you and others. Look at anger as harmless and it will stay that way. It can't turn into a monster if you realize it's not a big deal.

It's my hope as you read the following thoughts about anger - and learn some practical teachings about how to deal with it - that you will form a new perspective on what role anger plays in your life. We don't think of how valid and helpful anger can be. Let's welcome it, deflate it, and then let it go. It's the struggle of denial that gets in the way. To put anger in its appropriate place, we have to say, "Who gives a shite!"

# ANGER

Who gives a shite?

## Chapter 1
# UNDERSTANDING ANGER

*Anger is a Messenger – Listen to It*

What's the first thought you have in reaction to the word "anger?" Most people would say that anger is a negative emotion, something they would like to avoid and purge from their lives. Though the goal is to let go of anger, and experience life from a perspective of joy, the first step is to recognize and embrace your anger. What is it telling you? Don't fear anger – face it and feel it, and then let it go. If we ignore anger and shove it aside, we'll miss a true opportunity to go deeper into ourselves. If we are afraid of these feelings, no matter how uncomfortable it is to sit with them, they will only rise again, misunderstood and toxic to our health, happiness and the energy we put out into the world.

It's natural to have disagreements with people, and to feel angry about various situations in our lives. Know that anger is something you are going to feel at times. It is not your enemy! Anger is a messenger that can tell you a lot about yourself and how you are controlling your reactions towards events in life. We strive to express our emotions with the beauty of peacefulness and reason. When anger arises, it's a signal and reminder that you need to shift your energy. Stop, breathe, and think. Ask yourself - What does anger feel like in my body? How does it affect my judgment and emotions? What in my past might be provoking anger in my life? What else besides the thing or person, which seemingly set off this feeling, might be causing misdirected anger? How can I deal with the situation in front of me in a constructive and serene way that gets past the anger and helps me achieve what I want? Am I feeling frustrated and/or confused when I react with anger? It could be challenging to pose these questions to yourself when intense feelings of anger have been triggered, especially in a heated interaction with someone else. The best opportunity might be when you've calmed down, a little time has passed, and you have the valuable gift of perspective. Writing down the answers to the questions can be useful to gain more awareness about patterns of anger and resentment. If you have a greater understanding of your anger, you're more likely to be able to let it go.

Asking these questions begins the process of shifting from unconscious reaction to conscious observation. But to identify the root cause of all anger, we need to look at the cause of all emotional suffering: desire.

## Anger's "Chain of Events"

### 1. Attachment to our sensory desires

Our five senses tend to be the root cause of all of our emotions. In order to stop destructive emotions like anger from ruining our lives, we need to gain some control over how we project what goes on inside of us. The exact picture of what makes us tick may be hard to fully comprehend, but if we open our minds to change and discovery, we can transform anger into serenity. As we explore this idea further in these pages, think about your attachment to your senses – what you see, hear, taste, smell and touch – and how they create desires. This attachment to desires can lead to distorted reactions to life. We must want something more, beyond external people, places and things. That "more" is self-awareness and a connection to our feelings. It's the key to serenity.

## 2. Desires breed anger when they are not fulfilled

When desires are not satisfied, anger arises and grows. Not getting what we want - things, experiences, understanding, attention, respect or love - makes us angry, depressed and sometimes ill. During our childhood, we learn how to act to get what we want from the world around us. We are, not surprisingly, driven by desires for pleasure and will do anything to get what we want. God love anyone who stands in our way!

**3. When we live with delusion, we get angry**
Over time, we become very good at deluding ourselves into thinking that everything will be great, and we'll be happy, as long as our desires are met. The reality is that desires just keep growing and growing until it's impossible for us to meet them all. It's at that point that the anger surfaces and all hell breaks loose, often causing us to become desperate to get what we want. An addiction to our desires sets in, as if we were on drugs, and our minds become distorted, losing sense of the bigger picture. We just can't think clearly, nor understand that true happiness is not connected to external desires. It's all delusion, but that delusion is a very real source of anger.

## 4. When delusion rules, recollection is lost

If we stop thinking clearly, we lose the connection to our memories and self-knowledge. We forget about our past experiences, and how they have shaped us. Maintaining this link in order to understand why we are reacting in a certain way to events and interactions in our lives, is so important. When we don't have this insight to the root causes behind our emotions, we begin to lie to ourselves about the motivations of other people around us. We feel as if they are stopping us from getting what we need, and we get very angry with them. This anger can spread, wreaking havoc all around us, out into our environments of home, work and community. This profoundly affects the energy we put out, and receive back.

## 5. The loss of self-awareness can lead to destructive behavior

When there's deep-seated delusion as to what will make us happy, we may very well justify all kinds of harmful actions and outbursts. When your mind is colored by thoughts that are disconnected from self-knowledge and understanding of what is truly happening, we create a system of reaction and response to life that is destructive. This can manifest as daily challenges in our relationships, jobs and family dynamics. In their most extreme materialization, people can find themselves in very deep trouble, capable of anything, including acts of violence and even murder.

## 6. Anger's "chain of events" creates a pattern

If we are not consciously aware of this progression from our sensory desires, to delusion, to disconnection to our past, to the manifestation of anger, we will be vulnerable to outbursts and toxic interactions. Along with desperate attachment to our desires, intolerance, envy and pride will all lead to anger, triggering patterns of misguided thoughts, conditioned by our formative years. As difficult as it is to break this repetitive cycle, the good news is that you can! But you must be willing to work on it. Digging deep and really getting to the heart of what is going on inside of you, is key to letting go of anger and finding a more peaceful, healthy and ultimately happier way of cooperating with the world. When you address your desires, and see that you need much less than you thought you did from the outside, your life's journey will reveal that the true gifts are the ones inside you.

## *The First Step - Acceptance*

Never, ever repress an emotion. Osho, the great Indian spiritual teacher, said, "if you're going to be something, be it 100 percent". He shared that if you are going to be angry, feel it and welcome it. Be 100 percent angry! If you're going to be happy, be 100 percent happy. Whatever you do, do it 100 percent. There is great wisdom in this practice. How can feeling your anger, so completely and totally, be of help to you? The acceptance of this powerful emotion is the start of a process that can lead to a new way of dealing with anger and living more joyfully. It is not the anger, or the source of the anger, that is the important element. It is how we experience it. In accepting anger, we own it. We can then let it go and move on.

You may be thinking that if you feel your anger 100 percent, you will explode like an atom bomb. Your inclination is to not go to a place of complete anger when it feels too strong. Perhaps you begin to feel compassion for the other person and your sense of reason and rationality kicks in. Though admirable, you've actually achieved very little in the way of a lasting difference. The problem is that you've left the root of the dandelion in the ground. Anyone with a garden will tell you that every time you cut dandelions down, they come back. Even if you dig down deep, but miss the roots, they will still grow back and perhaps even multiply! Dandelion roots go right down to the core essence of their being, much like our emotions. And here's the problem - unless you eliminate something 100 percent, it stands a great chance of revisiting you. And when anger feels explosive, rising from deep inside, that is where you need to go to understand it.

## *From Anger to Enlightenment*

When you adopt a new relationship to anger, the benefits can be tremendous. You don't need to get angry to get things done. The most effective leaders on the planet, conscientious CEO's, great teachers, and other influential people show us this all the time. They know how to express their feelings – even anger – in a healthy and effective way, letting go of the cycle of blame and resentment. If they have an issue with their employees, students, or peers, they discuss it openly, with a natural flow of reason and sensitivity. When anger rears its head amongst people around them, these people are open, they allow feelings to flow, and then it's done. Admitting to your faults is another important aspect to anger. When you have done something that is wrong, and someone calls you out on it, you may feel accused. Own up to it, to both the other person and to yourself. You always grow from your mistakes and forgiveness is a gift, internally and to the outside world.

There are people who have devoted their entire lives to a deep and intense journey toward enlightenment, and to the mission of teaching others about these revelations. If you work with a teacher, they can help you examine the root of anger, receive tools to fully experience it, and then release it. A teacher can give you a mantra that will bring the emotions to a heightened state – such as that explosion of anger - then begin the spiritual process of letting go. If you decide to embark on very deep work with a teacher, they will say "go into isolation now," which could be to a monastery or ashram. Even if we are not able to enter a setting like that, the process that happens there, of working through anger toward enlightenment, is a good symbolic example of something that is within everyone's reach. As a location for people ready for a major breakthrough in their spiritual journey, these monasteries and ashrams are not a place to come to eat, drink and be merry! Sometimes students will be put in a cell for a number of days, allowed to urinate and defecate on themselves, fling their food, and throw huge tantrums. Then at a certain point, at a moment of breakthrough, the student settles down and experiences a truly new state of enlightenment and being. All the preconceived notions of how to handle our emotions have been knocked down by the process of going deeper and letting go.

How does this experience within the wall of a monastery or ashram, under the guidance of a teacher and a tradition that keeps one safe, apply to those of us who cannot go into isolation? What can we learn about the process of releasing anger? In that setting, the physical walls create a vortex of energy that converges to transform into enlightenment. When a student's anger is unleashed, it cannot go beyond those walls. The anger no longer projects outwards. Think of it this way – everything becomes that person. There is nowhere to go but inside the self, where a calmness and higher insight resides.

Though the experience of an intense retreat at a monastery or ashram is extraordinary, you can adopt these ideas without going into isolation. In your daily life, you can work though the steps of listening to anger, allowing yourself to feel it, deeply, then accept it and shift your energy. Anger will no longer be an enemy, but instead, an opportunity to focus your feelings and lead you down the path of peace and harmony.

When anger arises, it's a natural part of your wiring and system of emotions. The difference between someone who has achieved self-mastery, and a student, is that a Master gets angry and then they let it go, while the student holds onto the anger. The defining and powerful difference is that the Master's anger is, very simply, consciousness. When the Master experiences anger, he just watches it leave. A Master screams, "don't do that anymore," then he turns around and gently gives the person a flower.

You will always experience anger and sadness in your life, along with grief and love and happiness. There is no way around it. It is a "happening." It is not a "doing." We do not have control of when these things arrive, but we do in how we react. Sadness and anger spontaneously arises, and when it does, the Master lets it go. He is not attached. He is not inflated by pride or dejected by depression. It is just a happening. Everything arises, but then shifts and moves on, where it cannot control your life. It's the unconscious anger that begins to create pathways in your brain, creating connections that will just keep growing, never allowing you to get to the root of the anger. You have probably heard the teaching "get angry when you need to get angry," but the key is to not let it rise unconsciously. An enlightened Master can provide a model for how to use consciousness and awareness in reacting to all of life's experiences and emotions. Unfortunately, whether we want to admit it or not, there are many of us conditioned and programmed to only pay attention to some situations when anger is present. If we had a better reference point for love and joy, that came from an enlightened place deep inside us, we would know that anger will only close our hearts and feeds on itself.

People often keep letting anger evolve and surface in their lives. It hits their control box, which is not connected to the true and joyful consciousness they can embody. The heart fills with anger, holding on to it, and projecting it outward. This can go on and on until you learn to bring that anger back into alignment, letting it flow – and release. You will come to see that that anger is spontaneous energy, but so is love. If you realize that everything is energy, enlightenment is going to happen. Perhaps even in spite of yourself!

## Chapter 2
# THE FLIP SIDE OF ANGER

*Everything Has an Opposite*
What is duality and how does it relate to anger?
Duality means when an event happens to you
in your life, you can either go down one road,
which is the road of love and peace, or you go
down another road, which is the road of anger
and distress. That is your free will at work.
Duality is something that every person on the
planet lives with and it's based on the principle
that everything has its opposite. Every cause
has an effect, every white has black, and every
love has anger. At a certain point in your life,
you begin to see this pattern of duality. And
you can begin to bring the two parts together
in harmony, and address both of them as the
same.

Duality is always at our disposal. You can use your free will to walk down the road of love and peace more often. How do you do that? By doing nothing. Just watch what is going on in your life now. The next time you feel that you're not getting something you feel you deserve, or not understanding an occurrence that's happening, look at it. Look at yourself and watch where your emotions go. You'll see that desire and confusion arise in the form of anger. You may very well be comparing yourself with people around you. Perhaps everyone else seems to float through their life, with angels hovering and fireworks going off. You get angry when you feel the world is saying, "piss off!" to you, and that there must be something inherently wrong. Jealousy and lack of self-worth are seeds for anger. When you stop buying into the idea that other people's lives are better and start living your own, you can start breaking free of the heavy burden of anger and move toward happiness. Remember – "First one, then two." You must embrace the "one." That's you. Then you can connect with the world in a healthy, loving way. One plus one plus one plus one plus one equals ONE. First YOU, then two.

We are often caught up in being a "doer" in our lives, failing to value the "watcher" we should embody in order to experience personal growth. There is a simple way of becoming the watcher. Start with yourself and work outwards. Watch every one of your emotions rise and say, "Isn't that interesting?" Just acknowledge it, and then let it go. Don't say, "Look at that! What's that? What does it all mean?" If you do, your mind will take you places you don't particularly want to go! Just "watch." That is all that you are supposed to do. It's that simple.

Be aware that anger and frustration arise. It would be unrealistic to deny these feelings. They are part of the duality. Even a master feels anger, and all it's variations, because he is living in the duality. The difference is that he doesn't hold onto it. He accepts the gift. It arises and goes. That same process is within your reach.

## *Forgiveness*

The duality of anger also reflects in forgiveness. On the other side of anger, healing can come in the form of what we bestow on others. Though some circumstances challenge the idea of forgiveness, it is a gift to ourselves. Holding on to anger and refusing to forgive turns inward, in a destructive way, and keeps us from growing. If we work through a process of listening to anger, accepting it and letting it go, we can then address the source of the anger with love and compassion. What does the person who hurt you bring from their past that they could be projecting out into world? What mistakes have you made yourself that you can relate to? The duality of all things tells us that there is always another side to the coin; another perspective that we may or may not understand. The important element when faced with the choice to forgive is the fluidity of life. Hang on to anything for too long and it will only bring you unhappiness.

Rather than feeling like a victim and attaching to anger, when you forgive you acknowledge that we are all living our own stories, and they are all connected. We have more in common than you may think. Forgiveness brings us closer. Sometimes forgetting is even better! People often feel they need to forgive in order to detach, but forgetting what has happened to you, and made you angry, may also be effective in helping to let go. Go deeper and see how the Universe has its own will. It teaches us lessons. Forgiveness is really about accepting that things happen the way they are suppose to.

## *Service – A Way to Joy*

The duality we find in life and the choices we make along the way can be seen through the connection between the outside world and us. As we work on improving ourselves and achieving happiness and self-awareness, service to others is a path to what is rightfully yours – a place in the world that is meaningful and deeply loving. Service will bring you joy. By aiding others you're eliminating the five poisons within yourself – anger, jealousy, desire, pride and delusion/ignorance. Helping those who need your assistance, or are less fortunate than you, brings perspective. Service summons empathy and strength. It teaches us what is important and reveals that the things and desires that we've made so desperately important in our lives are in truth, not. The way to joy is much more about what we give, rather than what we acquire.

## Chapter 3

# ANGER'S MANIFESTIONS AND HOW TO HEAL

***The Physical and Chemical Aspects of Anger***
There are numerous studies about how anger affects our physiology. We feel chemical changes in our body from a whole range of emotions. National Geographic published an article on how love causes a distinctive chemical reaction in our brains. We find the same is true with anger. A sensory chain of events is triggered with anger, often escalating and making us feel that we're out of control.

Anger emerges with a thought. It all starts there. It feels as if anger forms within us, but in reality, we attract negativity from the outside world. Positive thoughts and outlooks reside in ourselves. That is our natural, true state. The key is to tap into this inherent potential and shift our understanding. External forces impact us and we develop our thoughts about them. We have the choice as to how they will affect us. When a thought sets off anger, and that chemical reaction kicks in, we are in a spiral of negative thinking. If we know how to stay in our enlightened energy, our thoughts can't take us down that destructive path. Meditation is a great way to learn how to keep our thoughts positive. Anger rises and falls away when you use meditation as a tool for changing your perspective. Becoming a loving person, an important goal in your spiritual journey, creates a state of mind that anger can't hold on to. When you are not in touch with the human fundamental goodness and ability to love – that we all have – the chemical reactions that are triggered by anger will dictate your feelings and actions.

Our anger can manifest in physical aliments and conditions, from minor disorders to quite serious illnesses. When faced with medical challenges, looking at anger as a factor is vital and informative. Many people are visited by cancer. I called it "visited" because that's all cancer is, a visitor. It's coming and knocking at your door telling you that there's a part of you that's angry. Cancer asks you to look deeper into yourself. Cancer, like anger, is a messenger. It communicates that you must change your lifestyle.

You draw to you that which you are. Anger draws anger. When there are enough little cells of anger, they change their name to hide. They then call themselves cancer. Cancer eats away at us, as anger does. An injection of love is the way to healing, no matter the end result. Tumors are your body's way of telling you that you are angry. When you let go of your anger, you become more conscious, and the things you are conscious of always change. It's the same with any problem in our life – from headaches to financial situations to troublesome family dynamics. We must be open to having all these things come into our lives, not to hurt us but to enlighten us. If we're not willing to listen to that inner messenger, we can become ill or some other state of dysfunction. Now is the time for all of us to take responsibility for what's happened in our own lives and in the world - and what will continue to happen - and start to change it in order to have a much more positive outlook.

Though we cannot predict or control entirely what the universe has in store for any of us, there's great inner strength available to everyone that can be very powerful in shaping our health and happiness. Go deep into your thoughts and find the ones that are angry. Only good can, and should, motivate you. If it is anger that has driven your life thus far, the cancer or other illness is telling you to stop. If you feel unworthy, the sickness is telling you to stop.

There are situations, manifest in both individuals and in the world, which seem to go beyond our ability to make sense of or see their deeper meaning. We ask why we, or our loved ones, become ill. Why are children suffering? Why are seals being killed? Why are so many wars fought? What sort of God would do this? He is trying to get all his children home, and will use whatever tool is necessary. As difficult as it is sometimes to understand, we must come to see that we can't interfere with the Plan. Go with the Plan and let life flow, like water. Change is always occurring, and resistance to it breeds discontent and disharmony.

## *Projecting Anger – How it Affects Relationships*

Along with the impact that anger can have on your wellbeing and happiness, the projection of anger out into the world has far-reaching effects. When you are processing your anger and learning to let it go, be aware of how it can touch others. Your anger belongs to you. You are the creator of everything you feel and every reaction you have. When you displace anger externally, it can manifest in a direction that causes hurt and confusion.

In the case of someone being the catalyst for your anger, realize that this person has come to enlighten you. You can learn from the feelings that arise when your buttons are pushed. The next time somebody pisses you off, don't blame him or her, just thank them. As strange or uncomfortable as that seems, you can be grateful for this person showing you the way to your enlightenment. You can only hurt yourself with a lack of understanding of this dynamic. Anger is an opportunity for happiness and emotional release.

How can we better handle anger in our romantic relationships? When two people join together it's a mistake for them to look at each other. Instead, they should look in the same direction. What do I mean by this? We need to value ourselves as individuals in order to have a happy and healthy relationship. If two people look only at one another, they'll lose sight of the bigger picture and will suffer. Anger goes hand and hand with the misguided expectations we have of other people. Looking inward, then out into the world, together, is how to keep anger in check. Once we stop scrutinizing one another, and take responsibility for ourselves, we can feel joy in a relationship.

When people have affairs, the physical body often has no conscience. We are all made up of matter and if chemical reactions fire-up, it's very difficult to control them. It is the same mechanism when anger rises in your body. You have to sit in that anger until the chemicals balance out. If you have a good teacher, you will learn how to more quickly defuse those chemicals and shift your energy.

In all relationships, remember these basic ideas for combating anger. Always acknowledge your feelings and be responsible for how you express them. Communicate your thoughts appropriately and as lovingly as possible, and don't blame others. Think about your part in the situation or event, knowing that pride and arrogance can get in the way. Stop and reflect before you react, and go deeper into yourself in order to let anger pass through and drift away.

## *Anger and Violence*

Though we think of violence as a physical action that manifests in a very perceptible way, inner, psychological violence causes far more damage than outside violence ever will. Violence in the world is merely a mirror of people's inner suffering. War will never stop until humans end the violence in their own hearts. The same is true for the battles you play out in your life. Those clashes exist inside you, and have to be looked at, but you must also address the external ones. A cease-fire, in effect, has to be called in order to heal your inner struggles. Much like the classic "chicken or the egg" dilemma, neither the internal nor external comes first. You can't heal unless you approach them both. If you spend all of your time fighting your family, boss, co-workers, society, and God, you don't have the energy to deal with the inner conflicts. If you impose some calm on the workings of your life, you can be still, focused and disciplined enough to bring peace to your heart. Your inner battle against anger is fought between the duality of nature - between the illusions of right and wrong, and of good and evil. If you are coming from a place of integrity, your mind, body, and actions are in alignment. In this state, you cannot be provoked by anger.

36

## *Anger and Depression*

Anger and depression are versions of the same thing. Anger is negative energy projected outwards; depression is that energy projected inwards. What is at the core of that energy? It is the consequence of the struggle between what you want, and what the Universe wants. It is the friction of you going in one direction and the Universe tugging you in another direction. It is you resisting the Universe's love for you because you think you are unlovable. If we fight this energy, which is the true force behind our lives, we find ourselves struggling with anger and depression, unaware of how to find the light and joy that our thinking won't allow.

Depending on how your parents taught you to handle this energy, you become either angry or depressed. If your parents were patient and forgiving, they probably let you throw temper tantrums and then sent you to your room to finish them. They tolerated your anger, so you learned to direct the energy outward. If your parents were not tolerant of your anger, telling you that they'd "give you something to cry about," they reinforced a coping mechanism in you – the suppression of anger. You may never have had a chance to even feel your anger, let alone process it. Well, like many people, your parents might have abused you, criticized you, and/or taught you all sorts of bad lessons. You are angry and depressed because you think you got a raw deal. You think that life isn't fair, so you suffer. You feel angry because you think your life doesn't make sense. Here is the truth - you hurt because you love/loved your parents and you think they didn't care. This is true whether it is your parents, God, yourself, or someone else. In order to move on and heal, all you have to do is admit to yourself that you really do love yourself, your parents, or that someone else. You need to get over the fact people don't act the way you want them to. Once you know what is out of your hands, you can take care of yourself. The love, attention and support you feel is lacking from the outside world must come from inside. Without that, you are vulnerable to anger and depression, due to external expectations defining who you are.

You can deal with anger and depression by surrendering to it, and realizing that everything is a lesson. You must recognize that you are not the Doer – controlling everything. You are only here to experience life. The disappointment you feel in not getting what you want can be healed, quite simply, by wanting what you get. Success is defined as getting what you want but true happiness, that has nothing to do with things or other people, is "wanting what you get." What is underneath your anger? Is it fear that your parents or God don't love you? Are you angry or depressed because something happened in the past that disappointed or hurt you? Understand that it was the Universe experiencing that occurrence, not just you. There is a higher force that absorbs and processes these incidents. When you understand that the events that made you so angry or depressed did not happen to you, that it was the Universe and its powers at work, then the energy of resistance fades away and all that is left is love.

The treatment for depression often includes medication. Many people need medication so that they can cope while they make a spiritual transition. If you learn how to process anger, depression and other debilitating emotions, you will not need it. Doctors over prescribe pills, and though they have a purpose, medication cannot get to the heart of who you are and heal that part of you that is damaged. Only by finding a route to your soul and inner core, will you transform your life in a lasting, deep way. Anger and depression are seldom banished entirely, but they don't stick around. The result is that you learn to feel your emotions, and then let go. This has a profound affect on your life and the way you view your place in the world.

When you have setbacks, you don't have to walk further down the path of frustration. You can stop for a moment and say, "Hang on a moment." You have to pause when you are in emotional or physical pain. Go within and experience your Divine nature. Life is a bit like a pendulum. At one end of the arc of the pendulum is unhappiness. At the other end is happiness. Isn't that what life is like, a pendulum swinging back and forth? If you become attached to certain outcomes, and try to avoid any strife or pain, the pendulum sticks at the end of unhappiness. If you understand that pleasure is the space between two pains and pain is the space between two pleasures, you will understand that the pendulum swings back and forth. If you trust that happiness always follows unhappiness, you will move through your life with grace and the detachment that leads to joy. We will feel anger and unhappiness in the course of our lives, but the goal is to not stay there for very long.

## *Anger and Grief*

When my wife Linda graduated to the higher planes, I processed my very human and predictable emotions of grief and anger in about an hour. Then I let go of them. I was not attached to the feelings of loss or unhappiness. Many people take years to grieve the loss of a loved one. The bond we feel with their physical being is difficult to shift, and we must be gentle with ourselves when facing these changes. What is unfortunate is that some people stay angry after a death, for years. Anger is one of the stages in acceptance of loss, but it is something you must let go of. Being mad at God or whatever/whomever you want to blame is denial of the natural place of death in life. It is all part of the same whole.

When you can understand that the soul is immortal and we never truly lose anyone, the pain is lessened. Linda is with me more than ever. I am in constant communication with her Higher Spiritual Being. She has not left at all. You can let go of anger and depression in relation to grief if you understand these are temporary states of mind. How long you hold on to these feelings depends on how attached you are to having life your way. Unfortunately, we can't control life or the universe - only the way we react to it.

## *Anger's Role in Addiction*

Addiction is depression, but backwards. What do I mean by that? Depression is a decision by people, either consciously or unconsciously, to refuse to participate in life. We see a lack of enthusiasm in depressed people. With addictions, there is an overflow of enthusiasm but in an unhealthy, misdirected way. Drugs, alcohol, food, money, people, places and things become the objects of desire and the desperation to have them, thinking they are key to blunting pain, is out of control. Anger that is not dealt with properly and lovingly feeds depression. In the case of addictions, the depression acts out and harms us. It covers up the feelings we need to work through.

The numbness of depression and addiction are responses to anger. Numbing ourselves acts as a tool of self-defense and protection, but is ultimately counterproductive, making us more unhappy and angrier. If we listen to anger, accept it and release it, a heavy burden is lifted. Otherwise, we look for outlets in the external world and addictions fit the bill. When treating an addiction it would be a huge mistake not to look into where anger resides within you.

A large part of the picture of why you are dependent on substances, people or things may be revealed there. What in your past made you angry that you didn't have the chance or the tools to express? Do you allow yourself to feel your anger when it comes up, or do you stuff it down and deny its existence? Does avoiding your pain, by turning to your addiction, delay the healing and happiness that you truly seek? Getting help is so important, and making sure that you dig up that anger, uprooting it permanently by taking on a whole new way of dealing with it, must be an essential element on your path to joyfulness.

## Chapter 4

# RELEASE FROM ANGER – EXERCISES FOR LETTING GO

What are your triggers for anger? The next time you feel anger surface, stop and observe how you got there. Are there situations and dynamics that you can avoid? What are the incidences – and reactions - that happen time and again?

When we can't derail anger, adrenaline runs into the bloodstream and causes the body to stiffen. We might stand-up as the spine straightens in order to defend ourselves, as in the fight or flight mode. At the base of your spine there's a little package of energy, that shoots up into your nervous system. When this happens, you think you need to defend yourself when, in reality, you don't. Anger fools and deludes us. The next time you find anger surging, try this:

1. Lie down.


2. Drink water slowly.


3. Put something cold on your temples.


4. Breath deeply as you will notice your breathing has become shallow or might even have stopped.


5. Leave the environment, if possible.


6. Try to laugh at your actions.

You need to work on letting go of anger as if your happiness depends on it, because it does! The 6 actions outlined above don't need to be done all at once, just one or two at a time. The anger will subside quickly.

If you wish to go deeper, and get rid of the root of the anger altogether, I suggest taking classes with a meditation teacher. Find someone who has had intense training and has achieved inner and outer peace in his or her own lives. You will learn how to release endorphins into your blood stream to counteract the adrenaline that is gushing into your blood.

There are many effective breathing exercises we can utilize to alleviate anger, combatting it when it arises. Our bodies react to anger, triggering very real and distracting sensations. The mind cannot think clearly when anger is present, and the body feels vulnerable. Proper breathing helps to balance us. It is a source of calmness and happiness. Problems, both psychological and physical, result from not breathing properly. This is often overlooked. Fear, anger, depression, and negative emotions can begin with, or be intensified by, improper breathing. Try this one:

Using the thumb of your left hand, press where the V of the index finger and thumb meet on the right hand. Press gently and hold for 10 deep breaths. Then let go and closing your left nostril, breathe into the right nostril 3 times and out 3 times to a count of 10. Repeat with the other nostril.

# SOME LAST WORDS ON ANGER

Anger is an emotion that forces us to look deeper within ourselves and examine our relationship to the world. In many ways, it is a perfect reflection of the idea that we have a choice when it comes to how we respond and react to events and people in our lives. That choice, if a positive one, can benefit our own peace of mind and higher consciousness, along with improving our relationships. If we can develop a new way of recognizing anger, listening to it, feeling it, and letting it go, we will have achieved a path to joyfulness. Anger's reach can be so destructive, whether in our personal interactions, or as manifest in depression, illness or violence. When anger becomes an emotion that flows through you, without fear, and then is released, your heart will open to the extraordinary potential of a truly happy life.